Where Do Monkeys Live?

tree

hole

nest

pond

cave

house

shell

sea

Where do monkeys live?

Monkeys live in trees.

Where do rabbits live?

Rabbits live in holes.

Where do bears live?

Bears live in caves.

Where do fish live?

Fish live in ponds.

Where do snails live?

Snails live in shells.

Where do puppies live?

Puppies live in houses.

Let's learn more about the Philippines.

Adobo